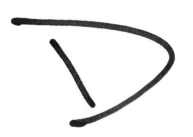

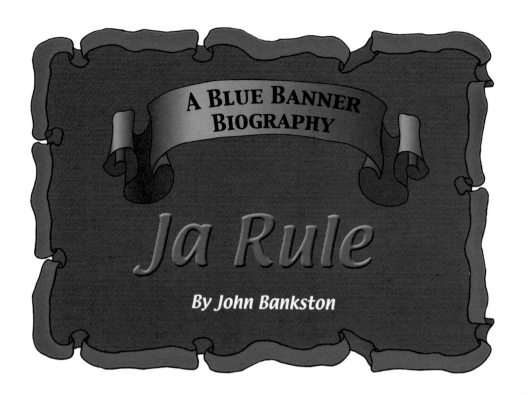

A BLUE BANNER BIOGRAPHY

Ja Rule

By John Bankston

Mitchell Lane
PUBLISHERS

P.O. Box 196
Hockessin, Delaware 19707
Visit us on the web: www.mitchelllane.com
Comments? email us: mitchelllane@mitchelllane.com

Mitchell Lane
PUBLISHERS

Blue Banner Biographies

Library of Congress Cataloging-in-Publication Data
Bankston, John, 1974-
        Ja Rule / John Bankston.
                v. cm. — (A blue banner biography)
Includes bibliographical references (p.   ) and index.
Discography: p.
Filmography: p.
Contents: Not a holiday — Serious hip-hop — The battle — Ja Rule rules — Hip-Hop movie star.
        ISBN 1-58415-221-4 (library bound)
        1. Ja Rule—Juvenile literature. 2. Rap musicians—United States—Biography—Juvenile literature. [1. Ja Rule. 2. Rap musicians. 3. African Americans—Biography.] I. Title. II. Series.
        ML3930.J14 B3 2003
        782.421649'092--dc22

                                                                        2003024039

ABOUT THE AUTHOR: Born in Boston, Massachussetts, **John Bankston** began publishing articles in newspapers and magazines while still a teenager. Since then, he has written over two hundred articles, and contributed chapters to books such as *Crimes of Passion,* and *Death Row 2000,* which have been sold in bookstores across the world. He has written numerous biographies for young adults, including *Eminem* and *Nelly* (Mitchell Lane). He currently lives in Portland, Oregon.
PHOTO CREDITS: Cover: Scott Gries/Getty Images; p. 4 Dave Hogan/Mission Pictures/Getty Images; p. 12 Evan Agostini/Getty Images; p. 16 Photo by Scott Gries/ImageDirect; p. 20 John Krondes/Globe Photos; p. 25 Tom Zuback/AP Photo; p. 27 Mark Mainz/Getty Images
ACKNOWLEDGMENTS: The following story has been thoroughly researched, and to the best of our knowledge, represents a true story. While every possible effort has been made to ensure accuracy, the publisher will not assume liability for damages caused by inaccuracies in the data, and makes no warranty on the accuracy of the information contained herein. This story has not been authorized nor endorsed by Jeffrey Atkins (Ja Rule).

CONTENTS

Jeffrey Atkins has come a long way from dealing drugs in Hollis, New York. Here he is shown performing with Ashanti, another artist on his label.

Not a Holiday

Standing on a street corner in Hollis, New York, Jeffrey shivered and waited for his next customer. He was 17 years old, a high-school dropout with a pregnant girlfriend, trying to make a living as he always had: by dealing drugs. Already he'd realized it was a dead-end street. Quitting dealing wouldn't just keep him out of prison, it would help him become a millionaire. Because Jeffrey was about to become Ja Rule; soon his whole life would change.

Jeffrey Atkins was born in Hollis on leap day: February 29, 1976. This meant his real birthday only came around once every four years. The parents of most leap-year babies solve this by celebrating on the day before or the day after. However, for Jeffrey there would be no celebrations at all. Not because of the leap year, but because of his family's religion.

Hollis was a neighborhood in Queens, one of the five boroughs that make up New York City. The area where he grew up could be rough and dangerous. To Jeffrey it sometimes seemed like the only people making any money were drug dealers.

Still, his mother Debra did all she could to provide for him. She worked hard at her job as a hospital nurse. His father seemed to work mainly at getting high—he was a drug addict who would often leave home for days at a time. Jeffrey was an only child (he'd had a sister who died as an infant), so even as a little kid, he felt like the man of the house. He did everything he could to keep Debra's spirits up.

> Jeffrey's mother did all she could to provide for him. In return, he did everything he could to keep her spirits up.

In the early 1980s, probably no one in music was as well known as Michael Jackson. His videos were everywhere; his music was played constantly on the radio. Jeffrey would watch the singer's moves. He'd imitate the singer's dance steps, hoping to lift Debra's mood when she was feeling depressed.

Music wasn't the only thing the future hip-hop superstar had in common with Jackson. Like the pop star, Jeffrey was raised as a Jehovah's Witness. This very strict religion doesn't allow its members to drink alcohol or smoke. They can't celebrate holidays, like

Christmas or Halloween. They can't even celebrate birthdays.

"It's tough on children," he later told *Rolling Stone.* "If you're an adult, you can make your own choices—you choose not to celebrate Christmas or you choose not to celebrate your birthday; that's your business. But when you're a kid, it's kind of hard to grasp those ideas when all the other kids in school are getting gifts."

What members of the religion do is witness: they go door to door talking about the church and convincing others to join. "It's called field service . . . ," he later explained to Paul B. Raushenbush of Beliefnet. "We used to always try to skip [it] because sometimes you had to knock on your friends' doors. That was embarrassing, to be in your suit and to knock on the door. You're cool in school and now you're knocking on a door in a suit."

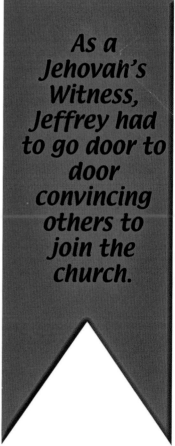

As a Jehovah's Witness, Jeffrey had to go door to door convincing others to join the church.

For a kid it can be very demanding, although becoming comfortable talking to strangers surely helped Jeffrey prepare for a future career in show business. Still, as challenging as his life was, it was about to get even harder.

Jeffrey's father was never much of a presence in his life, but when Jeffrey was seven, his father left for good.

"I haven't seen him in years," Jeffrey recently admitted to the *Washington Post*; "he might as well be dead."

> **Jeffrey's father was never much of a presence in his life, but when Jeffrey was seven, his father left for good.**

Although sometimes it felt like it was just him and his mother, the two were helped out by Debra's mother and other relatives. The extended family provided extra love and adult supervision whenever Jeffrey needed it.

"When I was little, my mom and grandmom did little things for me that always made me feel like we were doing well financially," Jeffrey told *Ebony* magazine. "Black people have a knack for that, making bad times feel good. They gave me a lot of strength."

Until the rules of the Jehovah's Witnesses ended everything.

Serious Hip-Hop

*A*fter Jeffrey Atkins's father abandoned the family, his mother and grandmother took up the slack. That changed as soon as Debra Atkins admitted to breaking a Jehovah's Witness rule. Occasionally, Debra had a drink after work with other nurses from the hospital. When church members learned she'd been drinking alcohol—a violation of church rules—she was disfellowshipped. This meant she had to leave the church. No one in the church was allowed to talk to her—including her family.

For Jeffrey that experience, and several others that followed, led him to question organized religion. Whether attending a Baptist service with a friend or looking into the Muslim faith as a high school student, eventually he concluded, "I'm thinking maybe religion is the problem." As he told Beliefnet, "It's a man who said, 'OK, you should go to this church every Sunday, you should go to the Kingdom Hall and go out to field service, you should go to the mosque.' . . . So, that's why I wear two crosses now. I call it double cross. I believe in God and not religion, because I believe religion is the double cross."

With or without organized religion, Jeffrey became more and more isolated. By the time he was 14, he too started breaking rules. But for Jeffrey it was worse than his mother's occasional drink.

By the time Jeffrey was 14, he started breaking the rules. In many ways, his life became one cloudy day after another.

"Life got a little different. Got introduced to drugs, started smoking weed, alcohol," he later admitted to the *Washington Post*. "Stuff like that changes a young person's mind, so I kind of went on the wrong road for a little while.

In many ways, Jeffrey's life became one cloudy day after another. His solitary ray of light was a girl his age named Aisha Murray. They were both in junior high when she transferred to Jeffrey's school.

"The first time I met her, I was getting off the school bus," he told *Ebony* magazine, "and she was the new girl in school. I hadn't seen her before and she was so cute."

But when Jeffrey tried to talk to her, she shot him down—embarrassing him in front of his friends.

"She tried to play me at first. She didn't understand who I was. She got into school and realized that I was one of the cool dudes, and that I was the man. So, I gave her a pass, you know. She had to learn the ropes."

Despite the early challenges, the two eventually hit it off.

She stuck with him—throughout Jeffrey's flirtations with drugs and crime. They continued to date when he began attending high school. John Adams High School was located in Howard Beach, the heart of an area the late mobster John Gotti considered his "territory."

"... we were very John Gotti–influenced over there. Actually, he used to call in bomb threats on sunny days," Jeffrey told the *Grammy in the Schools Careers in Music Handbook.*

"He used to say that the kids don't deserve to be in school on a day like this and call in a bomb threat to the school and everybody'd be out in the park playing and having a good time. Those were the good days."

By then, Jeffrey was restless to get out of school every day. He believed he was learning more out of

> **Despite early challenges, Jeffrey and Aisha eventually hit it off. They continued to date when he began attending high school.**

school than in it. As a junior he dropped out of high school. Not long after, Aisha became pregnant. Jeffrey realized dealing was a one-way street to either jail or the morgue. But he still needed money. He was certain rap was the answer.

Except, maybe Jeffrey wasn't sure of the question.

Aisha Murray is Jeffrey's junior high sweetheart and wife. The two are shown here at the 2003 Grammys.

By the late 1980s, hip-hop had exploded from an underground, urban phenomenon to music heard in more mainstream areas, from suburban homes to pop radio stations. Fueled by West Coast groups like NWA and East Coasters like the more political Public Enemy, it seemed like hip-hop was everywhere. Yet few groups were as popular as the one that sprang from Jeffrey's hometown of Hollis, New York.

Run DMC—Joseph Simmons, Darryl McDaniels, and Jam Master Jay—all grew up in Hollis, although they lived a more traditional middle-class life than Jeffrey did. Friends from childhood, they formed the group while attending separate colleges. From their 1983 hit single "It's Like That" to their crossover collaboration with Aerosmith on a remake of "Walk This Way," Run DMC was probably the most commercially successful hip-hop group in the 1980s. They were the first to have a record go platinum (sell over one million copies) and to have a top ten single. To Jeffrey, and to many other kids in Hollis, they were hometown heroes.

Jeffrey had been rhyming casually in his school cafeteria and on local street corners. Now he was serious. He took the name Ja, after his initials (ironically,

> *By the late 1980s, hip-hop had exploded from an underground phenomenon to music heard in more mainstream areas.*

Jah is also the Rastafarian name for God), adding Rule with more hope than certainty. Because in the beginning Jeffrey didn't rule. He didn't even come close.

"When I first ventured into music, it was all for the money," he admitted to the *Grammy in the Schools Careers in Music Handbook*. "I was broker than a joke and I was saying to myself, I'm tired of doing what I'm doing, I'm gonna get into music and make money."

> **Jeffrey formed the group Cash Money Click and quickly landed a deal with TVT records.**

He formed the group Cash Money Click and quickly landed a deal with TVT records. An independent record label once run from founder Steve Gottlieb's apartment, TVT Records began by selling sound tracks from television shows. Since then it's been the label for acts as diverse as Nine Inch Nails, Lil Jon & the Eastside Boyz, and the Black Crowes.

Unfortunately, the deal didn't lead to the success Jeffrey imagined. In fact, cash money never arrived for Cash Money Click.

The Battle

*A*t 18 years old, Jeffrey Atkins felt on top of the world. He was in a committed relationship with a woman he loved, he had a baby on the way and a record deal. And he hadn't even graduated from high school.

The good feeling wouldn't last forever.

The deal he'd signed with TVT Music wasn't much different from many deals signed by young artists hoping for a break. But Ja Rule would soon rebel against its unfairness.

"When you're young and you get into this industry," he explained to *Ebony* magazine, "you just see bright lights and big stars. . . . When it doesn't all fall into place, that's when you get a slap of reality that this is the real world and some people make it and some people don't."

As Ja Rule, Jeffrey's first job was on someone else's album, a common introduction for beginning rappers. Although today singles are usually released on CDs, they were once issued on small records called 45s. There was one song on each side of the record—the A side for the song the record company believed would be a hit, and the B side. Most of the time, music buyers

Jeffrey got his start as an unknown on a Mic Geronimo B-side single. Today he is frequently invited to perform at events such as MTV's New Year's Eve party.

and radio disc jockeys treated the B side the same way the label did: as a song to ignore.

Ja Rule's contribution was to the B side.

After their work on Mic Geronimo's B-side single "Time to Build," Cash Money Click began recording. In 1995 their single "Get the Fortune" was released. Played on the popular New York radio station Hot 97 and in clubs across the country, the group still never achieved the level of success present in Jeffrey's dreams. Irv Gotti was the song's producer. He earned his last name from Jay-Z as an homage to the late mobster, who like Irv had come from a rough part of Queens. When Irv Gotti left for Def Jam Records, it could have been a huge break for Ja Rule and the rest of the group.

It wasn't.

Def Jam was the place to be for many top hip-hop artists. Begun by Russell Simmons — brother of Run DMC's Joseph Simmons — the label had hired Gotti as an artist and repertoire executive. A&R execs are responsible for finding and developing new talent. The first new artist Gotti wanted was Ja Rule.

There was a problem. Jeffrey and his group had a multiple-album commitment with TVT Records. Ini-

> *Cash Money Click never achieved the level of success Jeffrey dreamed about.*

tially, the label refused to release him from his contract. In the legal battle that followed, Jeffrey lost the publishing rights to an entire album. In other words, the music he'd spent a year recording would probably never be heard by anyone. He was out of money. Even worse, one of CMC's members, Chris Black, was sent to prison. Jeffrey felt powerless as his rising career suddenly stalled.

It looked like Jeffrey was going the way of many young artists: a one-hit wonder with no money and no future.

TVT Records refused to release Jeffrey from his contract. In the legal battle, he lost the publishing rights to an entire album.

Ja Rule Rules

*T*he fight to leave TVT Records and join producer Irv Gotti at Def Jam consumed nearly three years of Jeffrey Atkins's life. In the meantime, his group Cash Money Click disbanded even as Jeffrey's family came together. His daughter, Britney, was born in 1995; his son, Jeffrey, arrived five years later.

By 1998, Ja Rule was back where he wanted to be— in a recording studio. However, once again his raps would first be heard on another artist's record.

There were few East Coast rappers more successful in the late 1990s than Def Jam's own hip-hop star Jay-Z. He'd released multimillion-selling albums, was running a successful clothing line, and appeared in some of the most requested videos on MTV. When Jay-Z heard Ja Rule's hook—a snappy, repetitive phrase that can mean the difference between a song's success or failure—he wanted it.

Jeffrey knew adding his voice to one of Jay-Z's songs could only help his own ambitions. In fact, when "Can I Get A . . ." was released in 1998, it was a hit for Jay-Z and introduced Ja Rule to a much larger audience.

Jeffrey is shown here with his family. L to R: daughter Britney, wife Aisha, Jeffrey, son Jeffrey, and mother Debra.

"He called upon me for the record, and it was no problem . . . ," Ja Rule explained to the *Washington Post*. "It was a good record. It was a big record. It was successful for both of us. Jay's gonna be Jay and Rule's gonna be Rule and that's the way it is." Jeffrey was on his way.

Roman emperor Julius Caesar's best-known quote, "Veni, vidi, vici," is Latin for "I came, I saw, I conquered." Ja Rule altered the spelling a bit, and in 1999 released *Venni, Vetti, Vecci,* which quickly conquered the Billboard charts. Ja Rule's debut solo album landed at number one on the R&B/hip-hop list and stayed there for three weeks. It also reached number three on the more diverse album charts. Eventually, the record would sell over one and a half million copies.

"I found out that the [music] industry is a little more about talent than I thought," he later told Grammy.com. "I really got into what I was doing, I fell in love with the whole art of making music, with being in the studio until four in the morning, and just working hard. I really fell in love, I grew a passion for music. And when that happened, I think that's when I started

> *Ja Rule's debut solo album landed at number one on the R&B/hip-hop list and stayed there for three weeks.*

making money. I started making good music and the money came."

Jeffrey's life immediately changed. He had money; he had fame. He was able to buy a large home in Orange, New Jersey, and to enjoy the "bling-bling" lifestyle hip-hop is famous for. He bought a new Bentley, expensive clothes, and a Rolex watch. Much more important to Jeffrey, he could provide for his family—stability that became part of the reason he decided to marry his longtime girlfriend and the mother of his children in 2001.

Jeffrey was able to provide for his family—part of the reason he decided to marry his girlfriend in 2001.

His second album, *Rule 3:36*, was a reference to John 3:36, and by the time it was released he'd developed his own rules for life. Part of his philosophy is called the Jordan theory, a way of looking at the example of pro-basketball star Michael Jordan.

Ja Rule knew that Michael Jordan was more than a successful African-American sports star. He was someone who'd succeeded in a variety of arenas—from commercials to movies. Yet Jeffrey also knew that the more successful someone becomes, the more often they are criticized.

Jordan was criticized for not taking more of a stand on issues affecting the African-American community—

some even labeled him a sellout. And Jeffrey Atkins, like many rappers, was criticized for his confidence, which came across to many as bragging.

"I look at Michael Jordan," he told the *Washington Post*, "I see a person who believes in himself so much, how could you not go with him? How could you not ride with him and believe what he believes?"

The album also spelled out Rule 3:36: "He who believes in Ja shall have everlasting love. He who does not, shall not see life, but the wrath of my vengeance… Pain is love."

In addition to tracks about parties and women, *Rule 3:36* includes a song called "One of Us," which was inspired by the 1996 hit of the same name by pop singer Joan Osborne. Like her song, Jeffrey's song questions what God would be like if the deity walked among humans.

Of course few people compared Jeffrey Atkins to Joan Osborne. By the release of his second album, his fans and critics seemed to see him as similar to one of two other performers. To whom he was compared depended on the audience. As he has pointed out in interviews, his music appeals to everyone from women in their 50s to kids who haven't hit their teens.

> *Jeffrey's music appeals to everyone from women in their 50s to kids who haven't hit their teens.*

By those over 40, Jeffrey's gruff, deep voice has been compared to the late soul singer Barry White, an icon whose music often formed a sound track for many romantic evenings to people who grew up in the 1970s. For younger fans—and many critics—when Jeffrey first stepped onto the hip-hop scene, he reminded them of only one man: Tupac Shakur.

A muscular five-foot-six, many people thought that Jeffrey looked and rapped like Tupac Shakur.

A muscular five-foot-six, Jeffrey looked and rapped like Tupac Shakur. In some ways, that was a compliment. Tupac's music created a bridge between the so-called gangsta rap of the '80s and the urban poetry that has been around for generations. With songs that dealt with the range of emotions from his love for his mother to his rage at society, Tupac was an inspiration to many. However, his murder in 1996 was seen by many as the natural conclusion to a life based on the tattoo that decorated his chest—THUG LIFE.

Not only has Jeffrey done a "duet" with Tupac (by sampling one of his songs), he also has his own chest tattoo: Pain Is Love. It became the title and menacing cover photo for his third album, although as a Def Jam spokeswoman explained to *Entertainment Weekly*, "I don't think he'd get a tattoo just for an album cover."

Like his first two albums, and *The Last Temptation*, which followed the next year, 2001's *Pain Is Love* sold well over a million records.

Despite it all, Jeffrey wasn't satisfied. In fact, he planned on retiring from the music business altogether.

When Ja Rule first became known to the hip-hop community in 2000, many people thought he resembled Tupac Shakur in shape and style of clothing.

Hip-Hop Movie Star

Succeeding in hip-hop is a one-in-a-million shot, a lottery ticket as tough to win as becoming a pro athlete or an astronaut. Jeffrey had found fame and fortune in the music world; now he wanted to gamble on another long shot. He planned to focus on acting in movies.

Making it as a movie star is easier for famous singers than it is for unknowns. Stars from Elvis Presley to Mandy Moore have successfully made the transition, as have dozens of hip-hop artists, from Ice Cube and Ice-T to Eminem. Of course there are no guarantees, which is why Jeffrey started out small.

In the beginning he was a supporting player, appearing in movies in which he wasn't the star. But after getting noticed in *Turn It Up* and *The Fast and the Furious*, he took a costarring part with Steven Seagal in *Half Past Dead*.

According to his director from *The Fast and the Furious*, Ja Rule is well suited to his new profession. "Rappers are natural actors," Rob Cohen told *Entertainment Weekly*. "Between their videos and their own on-stage

Although Jeffrey loves to perform in concerts, he plans to eventually give up music altogether to perform in another media: movies.

theatricality, it's very easy to direct them once you explain the language of film."

Despite succeeding in another field, in 2003 Jeffrey found himself locked in two feuds. He and rapper 50 Cent had physically fought when they were younger; and Jeffrey claimed to know DMX from his drug-dealing days. Now all three battled it out in increasingly violent lyrics. They also had their share of confrontations, including one in an Atlanta nightclub where it was wrongly reported that Ja Rule had stabbed 50 Cent.

His other battle was in a courtroom, as his former label fought with his current one. TVT won a $100 million award against Def Jam for breach of contract.

Despite it all, Jeffrey continues to make music. "I do what I do with my heart . . . ," Ja Rule told *Billboard* magazine. "A lot of artists make records to make money, not to make people smile or make hearts light up or to warm souls. That's why I make records and it's starting to show."

> **Despite it all, Jeffrey continues to make music. "I do what I do with my heart," he told Billboard magazine.**

CHRONOLOGY

1976 born Jeffrey Atkins on February 29 in Hollis, New York

1994 drops out of John Adams High School; signs recording contract with TVT Records

1995 contributes to Mic Geronimo's single "Time to Build"; releases first single with Cash Money Click; daughter Britney is born

1998 signs with Def Jam; contributes hook to Jay-Z hit

2000 son Jeffrey is born; first film, *Turn It Up,* is released

2001 marries Aisha Murray in April

2002 involved in collaboration with former CMC members; is sued along with Def Jam for breach of contract by TVT

2003 TVT wins $100 million judgment against Def Jam; Ja Rule is not penalized

2004 costars in two movies, *The Cookout* and *Back in the Day*

FOR FURTHER READING

Ex, Kris. "Ja Rule," *Rolling Stone,* March 29, 2001, p. 28

Hall, Rashaun. "Rapper/Actor Ja Rule Is 'Livin' It Up." *Billboard,* September 29, 2001.

Hughes, Zondra. "Rap Star Rules Hearts and Charts," *Ebony,* April 2002

Serpick, Evan. "Flashes," *Entertainment Weekly,* 10/26/01

Wartofsky, Alona. "The Golden Ja Rule," *Washington Post,* 4/29/01, p. G-1

On the Web:

Beliefnet: Double Crossed by Religion
   http://www.belief.net/story/45/story_4551_1.html

Def Jam—Interviews with Ja Rule
   http://www.defjam.com/artists/jarule/interview.html

Grammy Foundation—Recording Artist Ja Rule
   http://www.grammy.com/foundation/gits/jarule.html

Albums:

1999   *Venni, Vetti, Vecci*
2000   *Rule 3:36*
2001   *Pain Is Love*
2002   *The Last Temptation*
2003   *Blood in My Eye*

Selected Singles:

1995   "Get the Fortune" with Cash Money Click)
       "For My Chick " (with Cash Money Click)
1998   "Can I Get A . . ." (single with Jay-Z)
1999   "Holla Holla"
2000   "Between Me and You"
2001   "I'm Real"
       "Always on Time"
2003   "Clap Back"

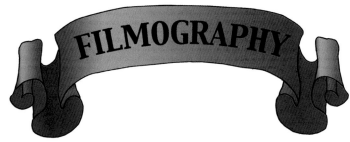

2000   *Turn It Up*
2001   *The Fast and the Furious*
       Crime Partners 2000
2002   *Half Past Dead*
2003   *Scary Movie 3*
2004   *The Cookout*
       Back in the Day

INDEX